Original title:
Beautifully Broken

Copyright © 2024 Book Fairy Publishing
All rights reserved.

Editor: Theodor Taimla
Author: Hanna Helimets
ISBN HARDBACK: 978-9916-756-64-5
ISBN PAPERBACK: 978-9916-756-65-2

Scarred Benevolence

In the quiet wounds of time
Scars tell their silent tales
Beneath the moon's soft chime
Our truth in whispers sails

Benevolence in the dark
Becomes a guiding light
Etching love in every mark
Where pain and hope unite

The shadows bear our grace
In intertwined embrace
Healing hearts in fractured space
With gentle, tender pace

Stars above, scars below
Reflect the love we grow
Through the tears and ebbing flow
In the scars, our courage shows

Gossamer Cracks

Fragile whispers in the night
Gossamer threads of dreams
Through the cracks, a gentle light
In starlit, quiet streams

Fractured hopes and broken sighs
Weave tales of strength unknown
In the spaces, through the lies
Truth's forgotten seeds are sown

Shattered prisms cast their hues
As shadows dance in flight
In the cracks, a heart renews
With every dawn's soft light

Ephemeral and fleeting
Yet eternally entwined
In the cracks, we're meeting
The essence of our mind

Luminous Veins

Beneath the skin, where light resides
Luminous veins ignite
In the heart where hope abides
A beacon through the night

Pulse of life within the dark
A rhythm, pure and bright
In every beat, a spark
Of undying, secret might

With every breath, we claim
The stars within our soul
In the veins, a burning flame
That makes the broken whole

We rise with every dawn
In light, our spirits drawn
Through darkness, we are reborn
In luminous veins, we're sworn

Graceful Disarray

With a touch of chaotic flair,
The world spins and sways.
In the midst of tangled air,
Elegance finds its ways.

Leaves in disjointed flight,
Dance upon the breeze.
In every jumbled sight,
There's a grace that never ceases.

Colors blend in disarray,
Yet beauty never fades.
Harmony in wild display,
Crafted in nature's ways.

Whispering Wounds

Silent scars that softly speak,
Stories etched in skin.
Wounds that form a mystique,
Pain that lies within.

In shadows, whispers grow,
Of battles fought and won.
Healing in the afterglow,
Wounds mending one by one.

Through whispers they convey,
The lessons learned, the strength.
In every marked array,
Resilience knows no length.

Imperfections of Light

In the flawed, the light does shine,
Crafting beauty from the true.
Imperfections intertwine,
Illuminating every hue.

Shadows blend with golden beams,
Painting life in varied shades.
Light weaves through broken dreams,
In dazzling cascades.

Perfect in their fractured state,
These beams of light embrace.
Every flaw they celebrate,
With a tender touch of grace.

Fragmented Serene

Pieces of tranquility,
Scattered far and wide.
In fragments they reveal,
A calm we cannot hide.

Shattered dreams of peace,
Glisten in the night.
In every shard, a release,
Of serene, gentle light.

Collected in the soul,
These fragments find a home.
Together they make whole,
The quiet where we roam.

Glowing Faultlines

Beneath the soil, a silent shake
The earth's own breath, a subtle quake
Fissures form where doubts arise
Glowing faultlines in our skies

In shadows deep, and moonlit nights
We trace the cracks by starlit flights
Through valleys cracked and mountains worn
We seek the light where day is born

Our souls are maps of vibrant hues
With faultlines running through our views
Though breaks may come, our hearts ignite
With glowing faultlines, there's still light

Celestial Fractures

Stars explode in silent flare
Cosmic whispers stir the air
Galaxies fractured yet remain
In broken skies, we share the strain

Constellations drift apart
Splintered dreams within our heart
Our universe, a fragile weave
In celestial fractures, we believe

Amidst the void, connections gleam
Bridging gaps where darkness teem
Through fissures bright, our hopes enact
In celestial fractures, we're intact

Splendidly Torn

Petals fall from blooming rose
Beauty found where nature goes
In splendid tears, the story's born
For life itself is splendidly torn

Mountains rise from shifting plates
Rivers cut through worn estate
From deep within, creation's sworn
Resilient hearts are splendidly torn

Through every tear, we see anew
The strength to rise and carry through
Our lives reborn at every morn
Within our souls, splendidly torn

Veiled Vulnerabilities

Behind the mask, a hidden sigh
In silent grief, the demons lie
A world of shadows, yet sublime
In veiled vulnerabilities, we climb

Through fragile whispers, we connect
In every crack, the light reflects
Our wounds, though deep, begin to heal
With veiled vulnerabilities, we feel

From pain and sorrow, strength is drawn
In quiet nights, awaiting dawn
We find our worth, though softly worn
In veiled vulnerabilities, we're reborn

Wounds of Light

In night's embrace, the scars ignite,
A tapestry of pain and might.
Through darkness, beams of healing bright,
The soul's own wounds, they take their flight.

In silence, whispers soft as frost,
Remind us of the battles lost.
Yet strength emerges from the night,
From ebon depths, ascends our sight.

O, fractured heart, let light seep in,
Where shadows end, new dreams begin.
In every wound, a spark that glows,
In every scar, the love life sows.

Delicate Disintegration

Petals fall, a silent grace,
In tender winds, they find their space.
From bloom to dust, a fleeting dance,
In time's embrace, a wistful trance.

Each fragment tells of moments gone,
Like whispers of a fading dawn.
In fragile loss, new beauty seeks,
A somber song, the heart still speaks.

Ephemeral, the stories weave,
In broken threads, our lives conceive.
From delicate disintegration,
A masterpiece in transformation.

The Beauty in Shambles

In ruins lies a hidden art,
From shattered dreams, where hope can start.
In every crumble, grace we find,
A beauty born of fractured mind.

Through broken paths, we walk anew,
In shards of light, the golden hue.
Our weaknesses, the strengths unseen,
In shambles, lies the grand serene.

The chaos holds a secret gleam,
In tangled threads, a woven dream.
From scattered pieces, wholeness rise,
In shattered forms, the beauty lies.

Breathtaking Fragments

Each piece a story, left behind,
In scattered trails, pure hearts can find.
A mosaic of the broken past,
Where beauty in each shard is cast.

In fragments, whispers of the whole,
The remnants of a striving soul.
From ashes of what once had been,
A phoenix of new life within.

Breathtaking are the frail remains,
In every loss, a wisdom gains.
In fragments, pieces find their place,
Completing art with tender grace.

Ruined Seraphs

Wings once pure, now fractured light
Songs of hope, in darkened night
Feathers fall, a silent cry
Below the stars, where spirits lie

Heaven's tears, upon the ground
With broken halos, they surround
Lost in echoes, dreams take flight
In shadows deep, they find their might

A chorus hushed, in distant time
Of ruined seraphs in their prime
Yet in their scars, a beauty rare
A story etched beyond compare

Cracked Twilight

The sky splits open, dusk reveals
Fragments of day, time it steals
In twilight's glow, the night becomes
A canvas cracked, where silence hums

Shattered hues, in evening's frame
Whispers of stars, they call our name
In broken moments, truth shall rise
Reflecting dreams in weary eyes

Cracked twilight bends, yet holds us near
A fragile bridge from fear to cheer
In each fracture, light and dark disguise
A dance of shadows, endless ties

Burst of Imperfection

In flaws, we find a gleam unseen
A burst of life, where shadows glean
Perfection's veil, it slowly tears
Revealing worlds beyond our cares

Embrace the cracks, the jagged edge
Within each fault, we make a pledge
To honor moments raw and true
In bursts of imperfection, grew

A symphony of missteps made
A tapestry of light and shade
In every flaw, a pulse, a beat
Imperfection's heart, so bittersweet

Jagged Stars

Across the night, with edges sharp
Jagged stars sing in their dark
A story etched in cosmic scars
Whisper secrets from afar

Glimmering shards pierce through the sky
In patterns bold, their truths do lie
A map of dreams yet to be chased
In jagged stars, we find our place

Eternal dance in space's flow
This astral ballet, hearts aglow
Each jagged star a beacon bright
Guiding souls through endless night

Splendid Scars

Within the mirror, whispers trace
Silent echoes of trials faced
Etched in silver, truth unveiled
Scars of valor, tales of healed

Courage defines the broken line
Strength reformed with every sign
Through shadows past, a rise anew
In splendid scars, a soul grew

Wounds that carved the heart so deep
Stories sung through nights of sleep
In every mark, a journey bound
Fierce rebirth where love was found

Mystical Mishaps

Beneath the moon, enchantments play
Mishaps dance in twilight's sway
Fates entwined with threads unseen
In realms where dreams and magics lean

Whispers weave through silent spells
Mysteries where enchantment dwells
An unforeseen serendipity
Mystical mishaps set us free

Through tangled paths of arcane light
Destinies forged in darkest night
Each twist and turn, a secret kept
In mishaps' grace, our dreams are swept

Divine Deterioration

In sacred places, time erodes
Heaven's echo in crumbled roads
Once divine, now faded gray
Deterioration in soft decay

Embers of the past alight
Whispers of a power bright
Splendor shifts to subtle hues
Grace that falters, yet renews

Each ruin speaks of history
Of celestial mystery
Divine in every weathered stone
Beauty in decay we've sown

Lush Ruinations

Among the vines where ruins thrive
Life entwined with pasts survive
Decay is lush, a verdant scene
Ruin kissed by nature's green

Forgotten halls where ivy spreads
Silent tales in flowerbeds
Life persists where time stands still
In ruination's quiet will

The once grand fades, now nurtures life
Peace found through the end of strife
In lush embrace of what once was
New beginnings rise because

Gilded Wounds

In silence borne, through shadowed grace,
A heart encased, yet fractured still.
The golden seams, both scar and trace,
Of battles fought with iron will.

A whispered cry, the night consoling,
Each tear a gem in moonlit glow.
Resilient soul, through pain, evolving,
In gilded wounds, the strength will show.

With every scar, a story spun,
Threads of hope through darkened loom.
A testament of light begun,
From ashes rise, dispel the gloom.

Fractured Blooms

In gardens wild, where chaos reigns,
Fractured blooms in silent pairs.
Each petal torn, yet beauty gains,
A testament to time's deep cares.

Beneath the stars, a quiet dance,
Frail blossoms in resilience.
Their tender hues, despite the chance,
Hold promise in their brilliance.

From broken soil, new life will spring,
A symphony of hope retold.
In fractured blooms, the heart will sing,
A legacy of strength behold.

Tattered Wings

Beneath the sky, where dreams take flight,
Tattered wings in twilight's glow.
A journey marked by darkest night,
Yet soaring still, through winds that blow.

Each feather worn, with tales imbued,
A canvas of the past's embrace.
In every tear, resilience brewed,
Against the storms, with quiet grace.

Through skyward climb, though worn and frayed,
The spirit finds its destined place.
In tattered wings, the strength displayed,
A testament of boundless space.

Cracks of Dawn

In shadows deep, the night abides,
Yet whispers hint of morning's grace.
From eastern skies, the light arrives,
To heal the wounds of dark's embrace.

A golden thread through cracks of dawn,
Awakens life with gentle kiss.
The night recedes, its spell withdrawn,
As daybreak offers boundless bliss.

Through waking hours, new hope is born,
In every hue, a promise found.
From cracks of dawn, our souls are sworn,
To greet the light where dreams are crowned.

Broken Halos

Beneath the golden light, they fade,
Halo shards of dreams betrayed.
Whispering tales of yesteryear,
Ghostly echoes draw them near.

In twilight's grasp, their sorrow hides,
Crimson tears on ebbing tides.
Their silent cries, a mournful song,
Broken halos string along.

Fragments fall like autumn leaves,
Heartfelt sighs, the soul deceives.
Angels weep in muted tones,
Forsaking love, they stand alone.

Veils of silver, cast away,
Night devours the light of day.
Once divine, now shadows trace,
Broken halos lost in space.

Enchanted Ruins

Where ivy cloaks the crumbling stone,
Forgotten realms, the winds intone.
Echoed steps on pathways worn,
In the ruins, dreams are torn.

Dusk beholds the magic's flight,
Silent whispers, cloaked in night.
Mystic charms, in shadows weave,
Secrets only ruins leave.

Enchanted spells on ancient walls,
Memories of distant halls.
Phantoms in the moonlit glade,
Ghostly dance, in twilight's shade.

Hushed the voices of the past,
Legends told in shadows cast.
Mysteries in ruins gleam,
Enchanted whispers, lost in dream.

Torn Whispers

In the silence, whispers torn,
Words of sorrow, hearts forlorn.
Through the nights, their echoes drift,
Tales of love and souls adrift.

Veils of shadow, secrets kept,
Tears unbidden, angels wept.
Vows once spoken, now but mist,
Fragile dreams that fate dismissed.

Stars bear witness to the cries,
Hurts concealed in midnight skies.
Every whisper, every plea,
Lost in time, like waves at sea.

With the dawn, they fade away,
Silent echoes of dismay.
Torn whispers, faint and frail,
In the twilight, pale and pale.

Veins of Fragility

Threads of glass beneath the skin,
Veins of fragility, we spin.
Life's frail tapestry, oh, so thin,
In the winds of fate, we begin.

Each heartbeat, a whispered sigh,
Echoes in the silent sky.
Every breath, a fleeting trace,
In the dance of time and space.

Fragile hopes and dreams confined,
In the labyrinths of the mind.
Porcelain hearts, delicate,
Bruised by love, tumultuate.

Silent tears in shadows gleam,
Veins of fragility redeem.
Through the pain, through the strife,
They find strength in fragile life.

Unveiled Flaws

Beneath the mask, truth is shown
In whispered winds, lies are blown
Cracks reveal a deeper might
In flaws, we find our guiding light

Shattered dreams paint the skies
Where silent tears meet knowing eyes
With every scar, our strengths entwine
In unveiled flaws, we form the line

Broken edges, hearts anew
In every loss, we start to view
Paths unfound in perfect strides
In unveiled flaws, our soul resides

Scarred Luminescence

Starlit nights on journeys scarred
Battles fought, hearts still charred
In wounds, a light still grows
Scarred luminescence softly glows

Through the haze of tears we tread
Holding on by threads we've bled
Each scar a map, a spark inside
In luminescence, we confide

In the depth of darkest night
Hope emerges, burning bright
Scarred yet shining, we persist
In luminescence, dreams resist

Broken Yet Glowing

Fragments scattered, beauty found
In broken pieces, whispers sound
Glimmers dance in fractured space
In broken yet glowing, we find grace

Through the cracks, light seeps in
Healing starts where wounds begin
In every break, a story sown
In glowing fragments, we are known

Heartbeats steady, though they're worn
In every break, we're reborn
With strength anew, our spirits grow
Broken yet glowing, we still glow

Splendid Imperfections

In the midst of flaws, we shine
Crafting beauty from the line
Where imperfection meets the day
Splendid shades come into play

Each mistake a lesson learned
In every turn, our spirits burned
Through chaos, order finds its place
In splendid imperfections, grace

Embrace the scars, let them breathe
In their tales, our hearts believe
Unseen wonders start to form
Splendid imperfections, warm

Elegance in Decay

In shadows where the petals fall,
A silent waltz through time's embrace,
Leaves whisper tales in ancient hall,
Decay and grace in tender lace.

The faded blooms, they softly dance,
To winds that hum a mournful tune,
Their beauty caught in fleeting glance,
Beneath the silver of the moon.

Ruins stand, grand in muted hues,
As ivy weaves its emerald thread,
A testament to time's old clues,
Where elegance and ruin wed.

Each crumbling stone, a story whispers,
Of days long past and love long gone,
Yet in decay, a charm twisters,
A timeless grace where shadows dawn.

Sacred Ruination

Among the shards of shattered days,
Where sunlight weeps through fractured glass,
The remnants of a sacred phase,
In silence hold the whispers past.

The altar stands in mossy shroud,
With vines entwining sacred stone,
Though broken by the worldly crowd,
Its sanctity remains alone.

Through cracks emerge the tendrils green,
Life bursting where the death had lain,
A blend of ruin and serene,
In holy ruin, growth maintains.

Splintered pews and tarnished light,
Reflect the grace in disarray,
In hallowed ground, the darkest night,
Gives birth to dawn's eternal sway.

Grace in the Gaps

In spaces where the shadows meet,
Where silence weaves its gentle thread,
There lies a grace, so soft, discreet,
In whispered words, by stillness fed.

Between the lines of what is seen,
In pauses where the heartbeats slow,
A subtle dance, so pure and clean,
The hidden grace begins to flow.

Through gaps of time and moments missed,
A fleeting touch, a sidelong glance,
Exists a world of quiet bliss,
Where beauty finds a second chance.

In eyes that smile with quiet gleam,
In breaths between the words we say,
Lies grace beyond the bold and seen,
In soft and silent interplay.

Radiant Disarray

In chaos, sparks of light arise,
A dance of patterns, wild and bright,
Through tangled paths and cloudy skies,
Radiance blooms in dusk and night.

The jumbled notes of life's own song,
Create a symphony so grand,
Though disarray may seem prolonged,
In brilliance, chaos takes its stand.

A tangled web of silver strings,
Reflects the light in shifting hues,
As order from disorder springs,
A radiant mess, the soul bemuse.

Each fragment, though it seems amiss,
Forms part of a celestial play,
And in the whirl of dark abyss,
Resides the glow of disarray.

Hallowed Cracks

In timeworn walls, the whispers seep,
Tales of shadows, secrets deep,
Through hallowed cracks, memories rise,
Solemn echoes of ancient cries.

Silent nights, with moonlight grays,
Reveal the past's forgotten days,
Each fissure, a silent tear,
Birthing stories caught in air.

Moss creeps slow on creaking stone,
Veiled corners, long since alone,
Hallowed cracks reveal their lore,
Mysteries from days of yore.

Whispers weaved in fractured rhyme,
Within the scars of endless time,
Guardians of secrets, old,
Hallowed cracks, their tales unfold.

Ephemeral passages carved unknown,
In every crevice, the past is shown,
Revered and cryptic, shadows cast,
Hallowed cracks, a bridge to past.

Divine Disarray

In realms where chaos breathes its form,
Beauty dances, wild and warm,
Through divine disarray, it flows,
The symphony of skies and throes.

Stars are scattered in haphazard glow,
Constellations shift and grow,
In the disorder, harmony sings,
Divine disarray, a dream on wings.

Tides caress the shores unknown,
Waves in disarray have grown,
Nature's mess, a pattern made,
In divine chaos, life is laid.

Twisting vines in tangled play,
Find their path in brightest day,
In every twist, a hidden grace,
Divine disarray finds its place.

Life's mosaics, random yet profound,
In the chaos, truth is found,
Through the complex, meaning threads,
Divine disarray, where spirit spreads.

Charmed Destruction

In the fire's fervent, glowing dance,
Destruction twists with fateful chance,
Wreckage charmed with sparks of light,
A paradox of endless night.

Chaos blooms in flames so bright,
Ravaging the silent night,
Destruction's charm, a siren's call,
In the ashes, beauty's thrall.

Whispers rise from shattered dreams,
Echoing through broken seams,
Destruction's charm, an art's embrace,
In the ruin, grace finds place.

Cinders fall in rhythmic gait,
Heralding a somber fate,
Yet in destruction, life renews,
Charmed by all that we must lose.

Through the rubbles, hope ignites,
In the dark, the future writes,
Charmed destruction holds the key,
To rebirth, a legacy.

Celestial Fractures

Stars once bound in cosmic bond,
Now break apart with tales we long,
Celestial fractures in the night,
Reveal a heaven, fragmented light.

Galaxies in pieces play,
Dancing in a grand ballet,
Fractured skies with stories old,
In each break, a truth is told.

Planets drift on silent threads,
Through the fractured blue and red,
Cosmic tears, though vast and wide,
Whisper secrets planets hide.

Through the ether, echoes spread,
Celestial fractures, paths to tread,
In the void, a hidden rhyme,
Songs of fractured space and time.

Amidst the splits, the worlds align,
In the fractures, stars do shine,
Celestial beauty, broken whole,
Midst the cracks, find the soul.

Divine Disarray

In chaos, beauty finds its grace,
Unraveled threads in wild embrace.
Each twist and turn, a dance so free,
In disarray, divinity.

Storms that scatter, winds that play,
Revelations in disarray.
Amidst the mess, a silent guide,
Where truths in riddles softly hide.

Order falters, plans may err,
Yet, within, there's magic there.
In tangled dreams, the heart will see,
The path to its own sanctuary.

Leaves that flutter, streams that sway,
Nature's hymn of disarray.
Whispers lost, yet deeply found,
In life's discord, we're unbound.

Through veils of night, the dawn breaks clear,
A symphony we long to hear.
In fractures fine, the light beams stray,
Embracing all—it's divine disarray.

Cracked Perfection

In flaws, the truth of beauty lies,
A perfect curve in fractured guise.
With every break, a story spun,
Cracked reflections of the sun.

No blemish hides, no scar unseen,
In shattered glass, a sheen.
Through fractures formed by time's demands,
We hold our worlds in trembling hands.

In mirrored shards, the self divides,
Yet unity within abides.
Each crack, a line of whispered grace,
On broken paths, we find our place.

Golden seams in porcelain clay,
Tell of hearts that will not sway.
Perfection need not be complete,
In cracks, we find a strength so sweet.

Through brokenness, resilience grows,
A testament to what life throws.
In imperfections, we reflect,
A vision of cracked, perfect.

Resilient Ruins

Amongst the ruins, life takes hold,
New tales whispered through the old.
Where rubble lies, seeds begin,
A testament to strength within.

Crumbling walls, yet spirits soar,
Through open wounds, we search for more.
From shattered pasts, dreams arise,
In resilient ruins, hope defies.

Time will test, and time will strain,
Yet beauty finds its way again.
In ruins' embrace, life renews,
In broken frames, fresh hues.

Silent echoes of what was,
Whisper softly of because.
Through ruins' grace, we redefine,
In resilient hearts, we shine.

Tattered once, yet never gone,
Through darkest nights, we see the dawn.
In ruins, strength forever lies,
Resilient, bold, beneath the skies.

Splendid Scars

Each scar, a story etched in time,
A verse within our silent rhyme.
Through pain and trials, beauty seeps,
In splendid scars, the soul deep keeps.

Lines of silver, wounds that heal,
Embodying the strength we feel.
In every mark, a journey told,
Splendid scars, both brave and bold.

From battles fought and tears once shed,
Life's tapestry, by scars is led.
Each line, a grace, both fierce and true,
In splendid scars, we are renewed.

These tender marks we bravely wear,
Echoes of the love and care.
In mended breaks, we find our stars,
A constellation of splendid scars.

With every scar, a testament,
To moments lived, and time well spent.
In life's grand tale, our greatest memoirs,
Are written in our splendid scars.

Serenity in Scatter

Beneath the sky in scattered dreams,
Where whispers cease to roam.
We find the peace in fractured beams,
And call the chaos home.

The silent breeze through autumn leaves,
Each rustle holds a song.
In swirling grace, our heart receives,
A place where we belong.

Among the stars, the night unfolds,
A tapestry of light.
In broken realms, a truth it holds,
Through dark, we find our sight.

In fragments, we discover whole,
The beauty in the pyre.
For scattered souls, a common goal,
To rise from the mire.

Mystical Disrepair

In ruins deep, where shadows play,
A haunting place of yore.
The echoes of a brighter day,
Reside forevermore.

The secrets that the silence keeps,
In whispers, old and gray.
A solace in the depths it reaps,
Where dreams have gone astray.

Through jagged stone and broken glass,
A story old and rare.
A bygone era's wistful pass,
In mystical disrepair.

The cracked facade, a somber grace,
Of time that's run askew.
Yet in its wreck, a sacred place,
Where magic must renew.

Ethereal Ruptures

In spaces where the light transcends,
The fabric tears so slight.
Ethereal forces start to mend,
The dark becomes the light.

A glimpse of realms that intertwine,
Through rifts, the threads do show.
Beyond the veil, a sight divine,
In ruptures, truths bestow.

A whisper through the breach so keen,
Of realms where time suspends.
Where boundaries are merely seen,
And fantasies amends.

Through broken skies, the stars align,
In cracks, the dreams emerge.
A cosmic dance in perfect sign,
In ruptures, fates converge.

Luminous Wreckage

Amidst the wreckage, light displays,
A gleam within the night.
In shattered worlds, a brilliant blaze,
A beacon shining bright.

The fragments of the past all strewn,
Reflect a golden hue.
An ember in the darkest moon,
In ruins, hope renews.

Beneath the ash, a fire grows,
Reviving lost domains.
In luminous wreckage, life bestows,
A warmth that still remains.

Through scattered dreams of broken glass,
We find the light obscure.
In every breach, a spark shall pass,
A glow forever pure.

Jagged Harmony

In the dissonance of night,
Stars blaze in jagged lines,
A symphony not quite right,
Yet sublime it intertwines.

Moonlit shards of glass,
Reflect a broken grace,
In jagged harmony they pass,
Through the silent space.

Uneven tones emerge,
From shadows left unturned,
Their jagged edges verge,
On secrets never learned.

Harmony in chaos found,
In echoes sharp and grand,
A jagged symphony unbound,
Across the starlit land.

Nature's fractured tune,
Plays in the night so deep,
Jagged harmony will swoon,
Till morning light's first peep.

Whispers of the Fractured

Shattered dreams in silence lay,
Broken whispers fill the night,
Fractured souls in disarray,
Seek a glimmer of the light.

Echoes of the past resound,
In the hollow, shattered air,
Whispers of the fractured found,
Truths too delicate to share.

In the quiet, shadows speak,
Words of loss and tales of woe,
Whispers soft and voices weak,
Where the fractured winds do blow.

Haunted by the whispered song,
Of a time that once was whole,
Fractured echoes drift along,
Through the corridors of soul.

Yet in whispers, hope is born,
Amidst the fractured, gentle flight,
Promises of a new dawn,
Rising softly with the light.

Radiant Cracks

In the surface, flaws reveal,
Cracks where light seeps through,
Radiant beams they gently steal,
To paint the world anew.

Through the cracks, a light emerges,
Brighter than the sun,
In those radiant surges,
New hope has just begun.

Each crack a story tells,
Of wounds and healing tides,
Radiant light within them dwells,
Where resilience resides.

Cracks upon the surface bare,
Glimmer with resilient might,
Radiant paths beyond despair,
Guide towards the light.

In each crack, a promise glows,
Of beauty born from strife,
Radiant cracks the heart bestows,
On the tapestry of life.

Splintered Dreams

In the quiet of the night,
Splintered dreams take flight,
Fragments of a broken sight,
Yearning for the light.

Stars above bear witness,
To dreams that slowly break,
In their splintered fitness,
New paths they start to make.

From the ashes, hopes arise,
Splintered dreams renew,
In the twilight skies,
They find a form that's true.

Every splintered fragment,
Holds a secret seed,
Of a dream resplendent,
To fulfill a hidden need.

Through the splinters gleams,
Echoes of what's near,
In the journey of such dreams,
Lies the path so clear.

In Perfect Ruin

In the shadow of a crumbling frame,
We find the remnants of a dream,
Eclipsed beneath a tarnished name,
Revived by whispers of a theme.

The bricks decayed with time's embrace,
Yet bind a story, rough and true,
Within the cracks, a fleeting grace,
A sanctuary born anew.

The ruins speak of days gone by,
Of lives entwined in twilight's glow,
Where echoes of a muted sigh,
Reveal the paths we seldom show.

In perfect ruin, we discern,
The beauty in fragmented lore,
The lessons in each twist and turn,
Through broken doors, we shall explore.

For every ending breeds a birth,
In rubble, hope will still alight,
The essence of a fractured earth,
Is captured in the softest light.

Shards of Serendipity

Beneath the veil of happenstance,
Lies fragments, glittering and bright,
A tapestry of flitting chance,
That guides us gently through the night.

In every shard, we glimpse a tale,
Of fortitude and fleeting sway,
Uncovering truths both frail and hale,
Upon our winding path, they lay.

The serendipity in our stride,
Composed of moments unforeseen,
Binds our hearts, their whispers guide,
Through hidden realms and worlds between.

Embrace the fragments that we bear,
Their beauty in the rough unknown,
For in their glow, we learn to dare,
To walk a path not walked alone.

So cherish every fleeting shard,
Of chance and wonder, wild and free,
For life, though fractured, leads us far,
Through shards of serendipity.

Blessed Imperfections

In the chaos of our untamed dreams,
Lie imperfections: blessed, bright,
Each flaw a star that softly gleams,
Amidst the calm of darkest night.

Our scars, the maps of journeys past,
Etched deep into our tender skin,
They draw the bounds of futures vast,
Where aspirations can begin.

Embrace the cracks that light our way,
Through shadows cast by past mistakes,
In every fault, a promise lay,
For every heartache, courage wakes.

Among the flaws, a truth revealed,
That perfect's but a fleeting lie,
It's in our wounds, our spirits healed,
We find the strength to reach the sky.

So let us honor every trace,
Of blessed imperfections borne,
For in their humble, rugged grace,
We rise, renewed, each golden morn.

The Art of Falling Apart

In every tempest lies a calm,
A beauty in the fractured frame,
The art of loss, a haunting charm,
A tender, softly murmured name.

As pieces scatter, hearts reveal,
The essence of a tender core,
In fragments, we begin to heal,
To find the truths we can't ignore.

The falling leaves, a whispered lore,
Of seasons passing, dreams that fray,
Yet in their dance, we learn to soar,
On wings of night that birth the day.

Each fracture holds a secret key,
To realms of wonder, veiled in night,
In falling, we are wild and free,
In breaking, find our truest light.

Embrace the art of falling deep,
For every tear, a story starts,
In shattered moments, dreams we keep,
The wondrous art of falling apart.

Whispers in the Cracks

Hidden voices softly call
Between each silent hall
Echoes flutter, shadows fall
In corners dark, we hear them all

In the places light won't reach
Messages on walls they teach
Secrets seep through fractured speech
In the cracks, their whispers breach

Through the stillness, whispers thread
Of words unsaid, of tears we shed
Mysteries in quiet spread
Stories lived and stories dead

Beneath the floorboards, whispers rise
Invisible to prying eyes
Past and present they reprise
In the cracks where silence lies

Fragments of Dawn

Morning breaks in shards of light
Scattered rays dissolve the night
Day awakens soft and bright
With dawn's fragments taking flight

Golden hues the sky adorn
Silent peace is gently born
Nature greets each nascent morn
In fragments of the early dawn

Whispers of a new day's breeze
Stirring leaves on ancient trees
Moments caught like memories
In dawn's bright, fragmented seas

Silent glimmers take their place
In the warming, waking grace
Fragmented dawn, a slow embrace
Of day's first light upon our face

Resonant Ruin

Through the remnants of the past
Echoes of what could not last
Ruins speak, their shadows cast
Stories held within their grasp

Once grand walls now stand in quiet
In stillness they defy the riot
Resonating with a silent diet
Of time's end and beauty's diet

Moss and stone in solemn grace
Hold the echoes, time can't erase
History's marks, they've left their trace
Within the ruins' ancient space

Resonant within these walls
Faintly, faintly, time recalls
Memory's voice through silent halls
Of once grand, yet fallen, calls

Shattered Reflections

Mirrors cracked with time's embrace
Reflect our past, a fragmented face
Shattered dreams in broken space
Memories too frail to trace

Pieces fall, reflections blur
In each shard, the echoes stir
Past and present, how they confer
In glass's fragile, silent purr

Fragmented scenes in shadows lie
Mirrored slivers catch the eye
Stories told in gleaming sighs
In shattered glass where memories hide

Through the fragments, truths unfold
Tales of love, of hearts grown cold
In shattered glass, their stories told
Reflections of the lives they hold

Glistening Scars

In the twilight's gentle fold,
  Memories of battles past,
  Glistening scars, stories told,
  Beauty in the shadows cast.

  Each mark a tale of survival,
  Beneath the armor, hearts beat,
  Strength in each new arrival,
  Finding peaceful, calm retreat.

  Through pain, wisdom is born,
  Cracks where light filters in,
  Brave faces wear the morn,
  Glory in the flaws within.

  An ode to silent warriors,
  Who bear their marks with grace,
  Their courage shines far superior,
  A testament time can't erase.

  Harbored by the night sky,
  Celestial, star-bound archive,
  Each scar a reason why,
  It's a map of being alive.

The Poetry of Collapse

In the ruins where dreams shatter,
  There lies the seed of hope,
  A fragile heartbeats' patter,
  In collapse, we learn to cope.

  The broken walls tell stories,
  Of trials, tears, and woe,
  Yet within, hidden glories,
  Await the light's soft glow.

  Each fragment bears a promise,
  In the quiet comes clarity,
  The end births a new canvas,
  From debris springs rarity.

  Chaos births creation,
  In shadows, visions spark,
  A dance of new foundations,
  Illuminates life's arc.

  Through collapse, we find art,
  The poetry in demise,
  A resilient, tender heart,
  Rises 'neath fallen skies.

Dazzling Detritus

Amidst the refuse lies glimmer,
  Fragments of yesteryears,
  Each shard a sparkling shimmer,
  Stories etched in fallen tears.

  The lost and the discarded,
  Hold magic deep within,
  Souls not easily thwarted,
  Turn waste to wondrous spin.

  Scattered dreams, a constellation,
  In the wreckage, stars align,
  A hidden, bright salvation,
  In detritus' design.

  Beauty blooms in odd places,
  Among shards and splintered wood,
  Grace in forgotten spaces,
  Where once, nothing stood.

  Embrace the dazzling detritus,
  For therein lies rebirth,
  A truth that softly invites us,
  To find our hidden worth.

Gorgeous Grit

In the heart of struggle's throes,
  Lies a diamond's true worth,
  Where resilient beauty grows,
  Rising from the dusty earth.

  Gorgeous grit, unyielding,
  Faces carved by time's hand,
  In their strength, a wielding,
  Of dreams that proudly stand.

  The path of stones and trials,
  Gives rise to fierce, bright flames,
  Fiery, unbowed smiles,
  That proudly speak our names.

  In every tear, a sparkle,
  In every scar, a seed,
  From hardships, pearls un-falter,
  Fulfilling every need.

  Celebrate our gorgeous grit,
  Let resilience be our song,
  In each struggle, we commit,
  To rise, unshakeable, strong.

Cracks in the Light

In the stillness of twilight's end,
Shadows of dreams quietly blend.
Light fractures, a mirrored delight,
Echoes of hope in the night.

Through the prisms of broken gleams,
Dance the whispers of fractured dreams.
Every beam a whispered refrain,
In cracked light, past and future gain.

Morning breaks with tremulous breath,
Scattering the shadows of death.
In the fractures, new life found,
In the light, our souls unbound.

Glimmer of the moon's soft glow,
Whispers secrets we'll never know.
In the cracks our hearts ignite,
Finding beauty in broken light.

From the dusk till the morning's rise,
Cracks of light reveal the skies.
Infinite stories, woven tight,
From brokenness, comes brilliant light.

Fragmented Beauty

In shards of glass, our stories lay,
Fragments of life's intricate play.
Each piece a memory etched in time,
A disjointed dance, a silent chime.

Scattered mirrors reflect our soul,
In fractured wholeness, we find control.
Beauty in chaos, perfectly flawed,
In brokenness, the beauty is awed.

Cracks reveal a deeper hue,
Unseen galaxies, a different view.
In each fragment, a star will shine,
Illuminating paths that intertwine.

The mosaic of our lives unite,
In fragmented beauty, we find light.
Stories told through every break,
In perfect imperfection, we partake.

Through shattered dreams and broken hearts,
We find our strength in fragmented parts.
Every piece holds a unique grace,
In fragmented beauty, we find our place.

Ethereal Disintegration

Whispered secrets on the wind,
Ethereal disintegration therein.
Fleeting moments lost in flight,
Dissolving into the endless night.

As the stars begin to fade,
Dreams in twilight softly cascade.
Fragments of what once were real,
Ethereal disintegration we feel.

Shadows dance in moonlight's veil,
Ephemeral stories they entail.
In the disintegration of light,
We find new stories out of sight.

In the ether, memories dissolve,
Yet within, new truths evolve.
Ethereal threads woven tight,
In disintegration, new worlds ignite.

As dawn breaks, the night's retreat,
Ethereal whispers at our feet.
From disintegration, hope is sown,
In the ethereal, we are known.

Grace in Decay

Silent whispers of time's embrace,
In decay, we find a subtle grace.
Each wrinkle, each line, a story told,
In weathered beauty, we behold.

Footsteps fade on aged stone,
Yet in decay, new life is grown.
Grace emerges in the faded light,
In every shadow, shining bright.

Leaves fall in autumn's breath,
In decay, we dance with death.
Beauty in each crumbling leaf,
In grace, we find our brief relief.

Time's erosion, a gentle friend,
In decay, beginnings blend.
Graceful endings, paths anew,
Decay transforms with a gentle cue.

In the ruins, flowers bloom,
Finding grace amid the gloom.
Decay reveals a hidden way,
In every loss, a new display.

The Splendor of Cracks

In broken lines, a secret lies,
A tale of strength through weary sighs,
A canvas torn yet full of grace,
Beauty etched in time and space.

Through jagged paths, the light unveils,
A heart that beats, a ship that sails,
In every crack, a spark ignites,
A glow that shimmers in the night.

Fragments speak in silent tone,
Of battles faced, the seeds we've sown,
Each scar a thread in life's grand weave,
Whispered dreams we hold, believe.

Eyes that gaze through fractured glass,
See worlds where shadows softly pass,
From every break, a bloom ascends,
A testament to how we mend.

The splendor found in cracks so fine,
A testament to strength divine,
For broken is not where we end,
But where the light can truly bend.

Shattered Elegance

Elegance in shards awaits,
A dance of fate in broken states,
Each piece a memory of time,
Lost in the cadence of the rhyme.

Glass that gleams in twilight's hue,
Reflecting hopes, a countless few,
Fragile dreams in quiet night,
Held together by the light.

In splinters lies a story told,
Of bravery in nights so cold,
Each fragment holds a piece of lore,
An echo of what came before.

In shattered brilliance, shadows play,
Creating dawn from disarray,
In broken lines, beauty persists,
A testament that life insists.

Through fractured elegance we find,
A strength in what is left behind,
For in each shard, a truth distills,
Life's beauty lies where fate fulfills.

Wounded Whispers

In whispering winds, the sorrows sing,
Of battles lost, and gentle springs,
A tear, a sigh, in quiet night,
Wounds that shine in soft moonlight.

Each whisper holds a secret shared,
A soul that cared, a heart that dared,
In silent words, the pain resides,
Yet through it all, the hope abides.

Whispered wounds, they softly tell,
Of how we rose, though sometimes fell,
In every scar, a lesson learned,
A beating heart, forever yearned.

Through wounded whispers, strength is borne,
In quiet dawn, a new day born,
Each silent cry, a bridge to dreams,
A woven path in silver seams.

In whispered wounds, the hope persists,
A gentle touch, the night resists,
For even in the shadows deep,
A whispered dream, we always keep.

Radiant Fragments

In fragments, light begins to shine,
A radiant glow, both yours and mine,
Each broken piece, a star anew,
In twilight's grasp, a vibrant hue.

Through shattered realms, the colors blend,
A spectrum where new stories mend,
In every shard, a mirror bright,
Reflecting worlds in tender light.

Radiance found in fragments small,
A beauty breaking through the fall,
In tiny glows, the darkness fades,
A dance of light in graceful shades.

From fragments lost, a tapestry,
A woven tale of mystery,
In every piece, a whisper heard,
Of journeys vast and dreams deferred.

In radiant fragments, hope is cast,
A beacon shining from the past,
For every break, a light emerges,
A testament where strength converges.

Ceramic Souls

In ancient kilns, we find our grace,
Fired by dreams of hands long gone,
Through fragile cracks, the light will chase,
The spirit's echo, life withdrawn.

With every chip, a story told,
Our hearts are vessels, full of clay,
For in these scars, our truths unfold,
We mend and break, then fade away.

Touched by flame, our essence sings,
In colors fierce, in delicate hues,
Bound by fate and fragile strings,
An artistry that's rarely viewed.

Softened edges, shards of time,
Ceramic souls, reborn in dust,
Each broken piece, a fleeting rhyme,
A testament to worlds we've trust.

Through kiln's embrace, we're purified,
A symphony of cracks concealed,
Ceramic souls, we've never died,
In every vessel, love revealed.

Glimmering Shards

Beneath the moon's soft silken light,
Scattered dreams by hands dispersed,
Glimmering shards in endless night,
Whispering tales of worlds traversed.

Each fragment holds a darkened past,
Memories of love and loss,
In every cut, a heart outcast,
A winding path our souls emboss.

They catch the sun and splinter hues,
Rainbow prisms dance in air,
Glimmering shards of life's old shoes,
Forgotten hopes beyond compare.

Through shattered glass, the stars reflect,
Mirrored moments caught in sight,
Each shard a thought, its own respect,
Glimmering through the deepest night.

A tapestry of fractured dreams,
Pieced together by the stars,
Glimmering shards in moonlit streams,
Guiding hearts to distant bars.

Resplendent Fractures

In the broken, light emerges,
Fragments glow with hidden flare,
Resplendent fractures, silent surges,
Beauty found in raw despair.

Cracks align in perfect chaos,
Mosaic tales of battles won,
Veins of gold in life's frail pathos,
Resplendent under the sun.

Each shard a splendor, delicate,
Whispered stories softly told,
In their midst, we resonate,
A legacy of lives untold.

Through the breaks, our essence seeps,
Golden threads connect our seams,
In resplendent fractures, love's heart leaps,
A universe of shattered dreams.

Embrace the scars, they are the art,
Wounds can weave a brighter lore,
Resplendent fractures heal each part,
Stronger now than e'er before.

Broken Prisms

In fractured glass, the light refracts,
A dance of colors softly cast,
Broken prisms trace the facts,
Of moments etched and shadowed past.

Splintered beams in range of hues,
Illuminate the darkened void,
Every crack a different muse,
A symphony both fierce and void.

Crystals hold a shattered gleam,
Reflecting truths in light and dark,
Broken prisms shift the stream,
Of life's relentless, ceaseless arc.

Within the shards, the cosmos lies,
Infinity in glass confined,
A universe within our eyes,
Broken prisms redefine.

Embracing cracks, the prisms blend,
Creating rainbows where they stand,
Broken prisms, hearts we mend,
With fractured light, we understand.

Fractured Grace

In the mirror, shards of light
Reflect the past, the future bright
A dance of fragments, lost, yet found
In chaos, grace is tightly bound

Each piece a story, whispered soft
In broken dreams, we still lift off
Find beauty in the scattered glow
Through fractured grace, we learn to grow

Time's gentle hand will smooth the way
Reassembling night and day
From shattered paths, a mosaic new
A masterpiece from what we knew

Delicate Shards

Broken teacups, porcelain fine
Memories traced on fragile line
In shards, reflections scattered wide
A testament to what's survived

In delicate shards, stories dwell
Of hearts that loved and arms that fell
Pieced together, one by one
In cracks and lines, the battles won

The fragments glint in soft moonlight
An echo of a past so bright
In every shard, a tale imparts
Of healing grace and mended hearts

Splintered Symphony

A splintered symphony of sound
In fractured notes, a song is found
Discord and harmony entwine
Creating music, pure, divine

Each broken string and silent chord
Adds depth and soul, a voice restored
Through splintered timber, melodies
Compose the heart's sweet remedies

The symphony of life's embrace
In splintered notes, we find our place
From fragments, compositions rise
A testament to countless tries

Elegant Ruins

In ruins, elegance resides
Through crumbling walls, the spirit glides
A whispered tale of days gone by
In silent stone, the echoes sigh

Each fracture tells a story new
Of time's hand and its tender cue
Beauty woven through decay
In ruins, grace, in its own way

From ruins rise a strength profound
In brokenness, our hope is found
A testament to time's embrace
In elegant ruins, we find our place

Crimson Cracks

In the heart's deep, glowing seam,
Love and pain, a woven theme,
Crimson cracks that softly gleam,
Whisper secrets in a dream.

Through the night, a silent tear,
Fault lines holding shadows dear,
Yet through darkness, they appear,
Radiant glimmers, crystal clear.

Hands that trace the broken line,
Find new strength, a love divine,
Crimson hues, a gentle sign,
Healing through the sands of time.

Within each fissure lies a grace,
In every wound, a warm embrace,
Crimson cracks in tender place,
Reveal the light upon our face.

An echo of what once was whole,
Binds together every soul,
Crimson cracks fulfill their role,
Mending hearts as tales unroll.

Tender Scars

Lines that etch upon the skin,
Stories of where we have been,
Tender scars, they start within,
Healing slow, life's gentle spin.

Each mark speaks of strength and fight,
In the day and through the night,
Tender scars, a glimpse of light,
Shining softly, ever bright.

Moments lost and battles fought,
Lessons learned and wisdom taught,
Tender scars that we have sought,
Bear the truth that life has brought.

Hidden deep or worn with pride,
Marks we carry, none can hide,
Tender scars, a shifting tide,
Shape the journey of this ride.

In their depth, there lies a tale,
Of how we soared, of when we fell,
Tender scars, they gently tell,
Paths we've walked and wished farewell.

Glistening Ruins

Amidst the crumbling stones we find,
Echoes of a distant kind,
Glistening ruins in the mind,
Treasures left behind.

In the silence of decay,
Whispers of a golden day,
Glistening ruins softly say,
Timeless words that never sway.

Broken arches to the sky,
Memories that will not die,
Glistening ruins, standing by,
Witness to our silent cry.

Histories in each fragment's sheen,
Past and present, interweave,
Glistening ruins, evergreen,
Stories we can each believe.

In the shadow of their grace,
Beauty time cannot erase,
Glistening ruins, in this place,
Reflect the light of every face.

Blessed Imperfection

In every flaw, a gentle trace,
Of beauty, time cannot erase,
Blessed imperfection's grace,
Lights the journey we embrace.

Through each misstep, a spark is born,
In broken hearts, no need to mourn,
Blessed imperfections, gently worn,
Guide us through the night to morn.

Every crack and every scar,
Makes us shine just as we are,
Blessed imperfections are,
The constellations of our star.

Acceptance in each battered dream,
Of what was lost in life's great scheme,
Blessed imperfection gleams,
Brighter than the perfect seems.

Kindness in each stumble found,
A softer path that's all around,
Blessed imperfection, profound,
Binding us in love's sweet sound.

Graceful Ruins

In shadowed halls where whispers sing,
Of timeless tales and echoed ring,
Graceful ruins, silent stand,
A testament to nature's hand.

Once proud walls, now draped in moss,
Echoes of time, a tangible loss,
Yet beauty shines in every crack,
Whispering myths from ages back.

Crumbled archways touch the sky,
Broken dreams that never die,
Every stone and every vine,
Tells a story, yours and mine.

Through shattered glass where light refracts,
Silent melodies, ancient acts,
In the ruins, life persists,
A sacred dance where time exists.

Walk the corridors of grace,
Feel the past, embrace the space,
For in the ruins beauty blooms,
In graceful silence, old tombs.

Whispers in the Cracks

In the silence of the night,
Whispers creep, just out of sight,
Through the cracks of timeworn walls,
Echoing through ancient halls.

Secrets buried long ago,
In the shadows they still glow,
Murmurs of forgotten lore,
Hidden truths forevermore.

Breezes carry voices lost,
Through the years their paths have crossed,
In the cracks where shadows lie,
Ancient whispers never die.

Softly spoken through the years,
Echoes bathe in silent tears,
In the ruins, faint and low,
Timeless stories gently flow.

Listen close to walls that speak,
In every crack, a tale unique,
For in the whispers softly cast,
Live the voices of the past.

Veins of Divinity

Through the earth, a sacred line,
Veins of divinity intertwine,
Carrying whispers of the old,
In the soil, legends hold.

From roots to heavens, paths align,
In the quiet, a design,
Mother's veins pulse and beat,
Underneath our wandering feet.

Sacred flows through land and sea,
Veins of ancient mystery,
In the stillness of the night,
Feel the pulse of cosmic light.

Every stream and every tree,
Holds the breath of deity,
In the mountains, rivers, stones,
Nature's spirit softly moans.

Listen to the heartbeat's call,
Feel the rise, embrace the fall,
In the veins of earth entwined,
Divinity in all we find.

Glimmering Remnants

In the quiet of the dawn,
Glimmering remnants softly drawn,
From the shadows, light will spring,
Whispered tales from long-lost beings.

Fragments of a bygone time,
Silent chimes, a distant rhyme,
In each shard, a glint of gold,
Memories of tales untold.

Shimmering in morning's glow,
Ancient echoes start to show,
Through the mist, in twilight's gleam,
Remnants of a sacred dream.

Hands of time may fade the light,
Yet the remnants still shine bright,
Holding whispers, secrets kept,
In the spaces time has left.

Treasures found in silent stone,
Glimmering softly, once known,
In the remnants, beauty stays,
Guiding us through fleeting days.

Paradox of Perfection

In flawless symmetry's embrace,
We seek a faultless guiding trace,
But nature whispers secrets, clear,
Perfection's flaw, we hold so dear.

The stars in all their myriad grace,
Show blemish in their vast, wide space,
For even in a diamond's glow,
A hidden flaw can subtly show.

A human heart, so prone to fall,
Yet rises in perfection's call,
Through scars and trials, we ascend,
In imperfection, we transcend.

In art, the brushstrokes wild, untamed,
Create a beauty, unrestrained,
Our paths imperfectly aligned,
Craft the perfection we define.

So let us cherish every twist,
In life's imperfect, gentle kiss,
For in each flaw, a truth reveals,
The paradox of life's ideals.

Flecks of Splendor

In morning's light, the world awakes,
With streaks of gold, and shimmering lakes,
Each dew-kissed blade, a tiny spark,
In nature's dance, a work of art.

Autumn leaves in colors bold,
A tapestry of red and gold,
Each tree, a canvas, wild and free,
A fleeting glimpse of majesty.

Stars like diamonds, night's treasure chest,
In cosmic fields, their light confessed,
Each glimmer tells a tale anew,
Of galaxies in midnight's hue.

Ocean's mist, a silver veil,
Each cresting wave, a whispered tale,
In every droplet, skies reflect,
A universe in drops, perfect.

Through fleeting moments, splendor flecks,
Our journey marked by life's effects,
In simple, gentle, fleeting sights,
We find the beauty of our nights.

Haunted Elegance

In silent halls where shadows drift,
A whispering wind begins to lift,
Ghostly echoes lightly tread,
Through rooms where faded dreams have bled.

Moonlight through the windows streams,
Casting pale, elusive beams,
Each flicker tells a haunting tale,
Of love and loss, both frail and pale.

Ancient walls, with stories lined,
Hold secrets by the hands of time,
Dusty portraits left behind,
Speak of souls now intertwined.

Curtains gently billow, dance,
Caught in memories' cold trance,
An elegance both dark and fair,
Haunts the dreams that linger there.

In every haunted, hollowed space,
Beauty holds a solemn grace,
For in the echoes of the past,
Haunted elegance will last.

Broken Mirrors

Shattered glass on silent ground,
Fragments' whispers, soft, profound,
Each piece reflects a broken past,
In fragments, mirrors truth uncast.

Splintered views, a thousand eyes,
See the world through fractured skies,
Each shard a tale, unique, undue,
In every break, a story's hue.

Glimmers catch the sunlight's gold,
In brokenness, a beauty bold,
For through the cracks, new light can stream,
In shards, the fragments of a dream.

Mirror's broken, edge and seam,
Reflects the breadth of human scheme,
For in our flaws, our beauty lies,
In broken mirrors, truth defies.

Pieces lost and pieces gained,
In every shard, our stories stained,
Embrace the fractures, hold them near,
For in our brokenness, we're clear.

Holy Helter-Skelter

In caverns deep of twilight's veil,
Where whispers of the wind assail,
Lost dreams cascade on silver streams,
Harboring long-forgotten themes.

The stars, like seeds, in darkness sow,
A cosmos where the wild winds blow,
Each pulse, a part of sacred art,
Unraveling the human heart.

Beneath the tides of time and toil,
The spirit finds its fervent foil,
Holy helter-skelter blaze,
Illuminating nights and days.

In chaos, roots of cosmos weave,
A pattern only hearts perceive,
The rhymes of life, so wild and free,
Are etched in all eternity.

With every step on twisted trail,
The echoes of a primeval wail,
We traverse the mortal night,
Guided by a spectral light.

Enchanted Entropy

Through gardens wild of gossamer lace,
Where time reveals its hidden face,
The blooms of chaos gently rise,
To weave a tale of sweet disguise.

Each petal holds a mystery,
In realms beyond our history,
Enchanted entropy unfolds,
A tapestry of tales untold.

Whispered secrets in twilight's grays,
The dance of dusk in cryptic plays,
From shadows born in starlit skies,
To dawn's first light, chaos ties.

In every breath of wildest air,
A harmony beyond compare,
The symphony of fate's decree,
Drifts within enchanted sea.

With tangled roots in myth and lore,
The universe we yet explore,
Unveils its secrets, dark and bright,
And leads us through the endless night.

Polished Pieces

In fragments of a shattered dream,
Lie memories of a world supreme,
Each shard reflects a distant past,
Glints of joy and shadows cast.

Through hands of time and tides of fate,
We gather pieces, small and great,
With care, we mend the breaks and seams,
To form the whole of what redeems.

The polished pieces, worn with care,
Their lustrous glow, a tale laid bare,
Each facet tells of wounds and scars,
Of battles fought and distant stars.

Within the broken, beauty gleams,
A mosaic of our hopes and dreams,
The art of living, all we seek,
Is found in moments bold and meek.

In lives repaired, a wisdom grows,
From polished pieces, love still flows,
And in the light of day's embrace,
We find our truth, our saving grace.

Sacred Shambles

Among the ruins of the past,
Where echoes of our glories last,
The sacred shambles whisper low,
Of distant worlds we used to know.

Through scattered stones and broken beams,
We walk the ghost of ancient dreams,
A path where shadows softly wail,
Their stories on the night winds sail.

In shambles, sacred secrets lay,
Of lives once vibrant, bright as day,
Their relics mark a time now gone,
Yet in their silence, hope is drawn.

From crumbling walls and floors of dust,
Emerges purpose, firm and just,
To build anew from remnants old,
A tale of love and courage told.

In sacred shambles, life prevails,
A journey where the heart unveils,
A legacy of human grace,
In brokenness, we find our place.

Shattered Elegance

In twilight's gentle, fading glow,
A mirror's truth, a subtle show,
Reflections break on floors of gold,
Elegance in shards unfolds.

Each fragment finds a place anew,
A dance of light, a different hue,
Graceful lines in chaos spin,
Beauty carved from deep within.

A silken thread through time does weave,
Stories told that none believe,
Yet in each splintered, fractured beam,
Dreams emerge from shattered dreams.

Silent symphonies of glass,
In broken realms where echoes pass,
Whispers blend in soft refrain,
Where elegance and ruin reign.

So find the art in every crack,
Where past and future, gently, track,
For in the shattered, gleams a light,
Elegance in darkest night.

Fragments of Grace

In the quiet of the morn,
Where dew-kissed leaves are gently born,
Fragments of a world divine,
Stitch the tapestry of time.

Whispers float on zephyr's wing,
Songs of grace the willows sing,
In each fragment, stories lie,
Woven 'neath a twilight sky.

Petals fall as moments fleet,
Mosaic paths beneath our feet,
In the space between the dance,
Find the fragments, take a chance.

Gentle hands that sow the morn,
Craft a world where hope is born,
In the pieces, hearts embrace,
Endless fragments of such grace.

Sculpt the dreams that lie in wait,
Fragments gathered, contemplate,
For in each shard, a world renews,
Infinite, in varied hues.

Dancing in Ruin

Beneath the smoky, silver sky,
Where ancient towers rise and die,
Mirrors crack and shadows loom,
Yet hearts find rhythm in the gloom.

Stars may fall and fade to dust,
Yet within this ruin, trust,
For in the echoes lost in space,
A dance begins, a fleeting grace.

Broken beats in silent night,
Trace the patterns of delight,
Dancing in the ashes cold,
Beauty from the chaos bold.

Winds may howl and oceans cry,
Yet through the tempest, we will fly,
Finding foothold on the breeze,
Ruin whispers, gentle tease.

Take my hand within this place,
Where world has shattered, leave no trace,
In the ruin's soft embrace,
We find a dance of tender pace.

The Splendor of Fractures

In the heart of crystal caves,
Where light through prisms gently waves,
Find the splendor, find the truth,
In fractures of eternal youth.

Lines that break and serpents bend,
Find a journey at their end,
Every crack a story frames,
In the light each one reclaims.

Silent valleys, mountains high,
Fractures carve the open sky,
Threads of light on darkness gleam,
Splendor found within the dream.

In this precious, fractured world,
Silken banners are unfurled,
Every break, a chance to see,
The splendor of what shards can be.

Embrace the beauty, deep and wise,
In fractures, truth is realized,
For in each break and every tear,
Life's splendor waits to reappear.

Hymns of the Unfinished

A canvas wide in shades of gray,
Where echoes of the future lay.
In whispers soft, the shadows play,
A song unsung at break of day.

The dreams unformed still drift afar,
Like distant, unassuming stars.
In twilight's arms, they find their spark,
A hymn composed by heart and scar.

In every pause, a story lives,
In every gap, the essence gives.
Completing arcs yet left undone,
A symphony just now begun.

The voids we fill with silent grace,
In unfinished lines, the beauty's traced.
Fragments float in the vast expanse,
Incompleteness deepens our dance.

We dance with time, our fleeting ghost,
A hymn for those who seek, engrossed.
The unfinished tale a treasure strove,
In whispered hymns of dreams, we rove.

The Radiance of Ruins

In ruins, light finds hidden ways,
To thread through cracks where shadows play.
A temple broken tells its tale,
Of time's embrace where dreams prevail.

The silent stones, they softly speak,
In languid tones, a strength they leak.
The remnants glow in twilight's hold,
A warmth within the tales of old.

The winds of change caress each scar,
And lift the ashes off the char.
In ruins' heart, the secrets beam,
A radiant, unending dream.

Each shattered piece, a tale untold,
A glimmering light in history's fold.
In every fragment, hope does shine,
Eternal rays on past's decline.

For in the ruins, dreams reside,
A radiance where shadows hide.
The fallen stones, a legacy,
Of bright tomorrows left to see.

Pristine Imperfections

In every flaw, a beauty grows,
A hidden light that softly glows.
Imperfect lines, a gentle grace,
A story etched on life's embrace.

The cracks reveal a strength unknown,
Where whispered winds of change have blown.
Each blemish tells a tale unique,
In pristine flaws, the truth we seek.

The broken pieces fit so well,
In every scar, a tale can dwell.
Unpolished gems, they shine more true,
For in each flaw, we find our hue.

Embrace the curves and edges raw,
In imperfections, find the awe.
For life's a tapestry of threads,
Where perfect lies with flaws are wed.

The beauty lies in incomplete,
In misses found, we find we're meet.
In pristine imperfections' glow,
The depth of life, in flaws, we know.

Flecks of Splendor

In simple things, the splendor lies,
In flecks of gold, beneath clear skies.
A dewdrop on a blade of grass,
A moment's dream in life's compass.

The whispers of the morning's dew,
In fleeting moments, beauty's true.
The smallest flecks of shining grace,
Adorn the dawn with bright embrace.

Through quiet streams, the gleam does flow,
In silent woods, the splendors grow.
The tiny fireflies' soft ballet,
Illuminate the twilight's gray.

Each heartbeat holds a spark divine,
In smallest breath, the flecks align.
In every glance, a spark does mend,
A silent fleck of light to send.

The splendor lies in eyes that see,
The flecks of light in you and me.
In moments brief yet deeply felt,
Through flecks of splendor, hearts do melt.

Resilient Echoes

In shadows deep, where sorrows dwell,
A heart beats strong, a tale to tell.
Through whispers dark, and twilight's song,
Resilient echoes carry on.

With every step, through storm and night,
A soul takes flight, in boundless might.
No chains can bind, no fear can stay,
For echoes resilient, forge the way.

Mountains high, valleys low,
The echoes rise, and onward go.
Through trials hard, and tempests wide,
In echoes strong, we take our stride.

For hearts that break, and mends that mend,
Echoes of strength, forever send.
In past and future, 'neath the sky,
Resilient echoes, never die.

Broken Euphoria

A shattered dream, of bliss once known,
In broken euphoria, seeds are sown.
Through fractured light, in twilight's hue,
A dance of shadows, starts anew.

In moments lost, yet memories cling,
Of fleeting joy, and sorrow's sting.
The shards of laughter, echo still,
In empty rooms, they haunt and fill.

Through tears that fall, and smiles that fade,
The broken euphoria, gently laid.
In silence loud, in whispers mild,
The heart's dark corners, are beguiled.

Yet in the fragments, scattered bright,
A hope emerges, in the night.
From broken pieces, light will soar,
Euphoria, yet reborn once more.

Elegance of the Damaged

In wounds that scar, a beauty lies,
An elegance no time belies.
For in the cracks, the light still gleams,
A testament to broken dreams.

The damaged heart, its beats profound,
In sorrow's dance, an art is found.
Through every tear, a story spun,
Of battles fought, and victories won.

In shattered glass, reflections play,
Of hopes and fears, night into day.
The elegance, in damage wrought,
A tale of love and lessons taught.

For every pain, a wisdom grows,
In every scar, the beauty shows.
The damaged soul, a work of art,
With elegance, and tender heart.

Milton Keynes UK
Ingram Content Group UK Ltd.
UKHW050131270624
444593UK00005BA/64